"There remains a serious difficulty with the summary dismissal of all Algonquian testimony regarding the behaviour of persons identified as windigo...."

- **Robert A. Brightman (The Windigo in the Material World)**

BEFORE WE GET STARTED..........

A quick search of the word "Wendigo" will show you first-hand that the Wendigo is more than just the stuff of folklore. It is one of those rather extraordinary cryptid creatures that have descended fully to the psyche of those who know it. It is a madness-inducing creature. In a rather counterintuitive, or if I may use the word crazy move, I followed the trails of the Wendigo down the deep abyss of the internet, newspapers, books, and every other resource I could find. This crazed search for the spirit of madness revealed many things to me, many of which I feel obliged to share within the pages of this book.

The Wendigo is a creature, or do I say a legend, that was born from human feelings and emotions that many of us would rather avoid — greed, hunger, and despair. It is a creature that dwells in the darkest parts of us, only to emerge in a real-life form when we least expect it. I am not saying that the Wendigo is an illusion; far from it. What I intend to communicate to you before you delve deep into this book is that, indeed, the Wendigo is a creature that can and does take over the mind. It is an anthropophagous monster that exhibits such wild behaviours and has grotesque physical

WENDIGO

THE MADNESS SPIRIT

Contents

features that inspire fear even before it acts. The creature is perceived to have spiritual and physical power that allows it to conquer its victims completely.

The mere mention of the Wendigo has inspired fear and sent unnatural shivers down the spines of those at the behest of the legend, precisely the peoples of the Americas. The tales are enigmatic and captivating, yet slightly elusive, leaving a lot to wonder for those who are curious about the hidden gems of the universe.

Despite the significant strides that we continue to make in terms of technology and innovation, we are still slaves to our primal instincts, and the Wendigo controls one of those deepest instincts — hunger. And it is precisely for this reason that the Wendigo has become more than just a monster; it is a reflection of humanity's basest desires and primal instincts, a manifestation of our animalistic tendencies and of the deepest fears that we feel. The Wendigo is a symbol of how hunger and greed transform even the best of us into something unrecognizable, something short of a monster. While this work is not an attempt at recreating William Golding's Lord of the Flies' thematic preoccupation, we will be exploring some stories that are based on the premise of what a person can become in the face of hunger.

It should be noted by the reader, that this book, while employing several elements of storytelling and folklore, is not a work of fiction. Over time, the Wendigo has emerged from deep in the Plains to contemporary American Literature. While I am not one to pass moral judgments on creative works, I am of the opinion that these popular culture depictions of the creature, have somewhat created a narrative around the creature that removes a lot of its natural wonder. As is typical of works of fiction, the imagination of the author gets in the way of the facts and the legend. There can be over-exaggeration of physical attributes and the general effects that the creature being depicted has on human beings. Yet, these works of fiction offer us some creative map through which we can read the Wendigo.

The Wendigo has been the object of the fascination of hunters, explorers, storytellers, and cynics alike. It is time to bring the creature out of the shroud of secrecy that has kept it hidden from those who can't look too deeply. I have done the work for you, and I will say this to you before you turn the next page: This book is your portal into the world of the Wendigo – a world where the boundaries of reality and myths oftentimes blur. But as we embark on this journey together, I implore you to trust yourself and trust your instincts. It is only by trusting yourself that you can make the most of the time that you will spend flipping through the pages of this book. Whatever conclusions you come to at the end of the last page are yours alone to make. All I can promise is a noble attempt at better understanding the world around us. This time through the bloody and tattered lips of the Wendigo.

As you turn the pages, you will encounter tales of terror and heroism, monstrous transformations, and epic battles against the Wendigo's curse. But remember, this book is not just a collection of stories; it is an exploration of the human experience and of our innermost desires.

Chapter 1

A CITATION OF THE WENDIGO

"There is such a singular, strange, incomprehensible contradictoriness in almost all these cases, and many I have heard, that I do most verily believe they are denunciations, witch or wizardisms: in any other manner they are not to be rationally accounted for ..."

-   George Nelson

Aside from doing the good work of spreading the gospel and sharing messages of goodwill across the world, there is one thing that we often overlook in the lives of missionaries. Missionaries, in the course of their work, often encounter a lot of cultural phenomena that are vastly different from what they know or are used to. And I am not just talking about new food or festivals. I am referring to spirits and legends as well. Sometimes, for fear of ridicule or embarrassing the church, these missionaries sometimes keep these extraordinary experiences to themselves, unwilling to share what they have seen or experienced. It almost became an unspoken rule of missionaries not to give credence to or acknowledge the legends of the people they are attempting to proselytize. For one, entertaining such stories might cast doubts around the message of the Church not just in the minds of new converts but also ardent members of the church and the missionaries themselves.

Thankfully, for every rule, there is an exception. As it relates to the story of the Wendigo, the exception was Paul Le Jeune, a French missionary who is credited with the first written account of the Wendigo. In 1636, Paul Le Jeune was working as a Jesuit missionary among the Algonquin people in an area now called Quebec today. Le Jeune was ordained as a priest in 1632 and subsequently posted to New France, the territory that was colonized by France in North America. Reports state that although Le Jeune had not requested the posting, he was more than happy to obey the request to serve there. Le Jeune embarked on a rather difficult voyage to his post and arrived in Tadoussac on the eighteenth day of June 1632. In order to succeed in his mission of bringing catholicism to the Native American tribes, Le Jeune, who was the Superior of the Jesuit mission, encouraged the missionaries to learn the language and customs of the Native Americans. These allowed them to interact more with the locals and be able to convert them. One of such local interactions led to an account in a 1636 report by Paul Le Jeune about a woman who warns of an atchen (Wendigo) that ate some member of the tribe. According to the report, the woman was fearful that the beast would eat more people if it were not "called elsewhere."

However, there is another written reference to the creature that predates Le-Jeune's report of the creature. The earliest reference to the creature seems to be from an entry in the Powhatan Dictionary appended to in Stratchey's *Historie of Travell in Virginia Britania* published in 1612 according to Robert A. Brightman. In his work titled *The Windigo in the Material World,* he writes:

> "The windigo complex consists minimally of Algonquian beliefs in spiritually empowered anthropophagous monsters, Algonquian beliefs   that human beings can become such monsters, and cases in which Algonquians experienced and sometimes acted upon cannibal ideation"

The wendigo is a creature of many names and a single season. Wendigo, also written as windigo, *wiindigoo, wintiko, wheetigo, windikouk, wi'ntsigo, wi'tigo,* or *wittikka,* is a monster whose origins are traceable to the traditions and legends of the North American Algonquian speaking tribes. It is also called *atchen* (the term used in Le Jeune's report), *chenoo, kewok,* or *mhuwe.* Some authors have offered a logical explanation for the differing identities of the Wendigo: they are of the opinion that the different kinds of

Wendigo described by people are one and the same creature at different stages of their life cycle.

Wendigo is often associated with the grimness and grayness of the Winter and is said to only make an appearance during periods of extreme cold. Like its many names, the Wendigo has different identities as well. Sometimes it is identified as a beast that stalks and eats human beings. Other times, the Wendigo is a spirit that can possess human beings and cause them to turn into cannibals. The winter monster is an evil spirit that can invoke feelings of insatiable hunger and greed in human beings, leading them to kill and eat other people. A person under the influence has no control over their senses and can commit atrocities such as murder when under the influence of the spirit.

The Origin and Geography of the Wendigo

If you asked the question of where the Wendigo came from, the answer you would get depends largely on who you were asking. But since you are reading this book, I will give you all possible answers there are to the question of the origin of the Wendigo.

Algonquian Native American legend holds that the Wendigo is a scary beast that surfaces during the winter to devour human flesh. This winter cannibal is said to have evolved from a hunter who got lost in the forests. The man became intensely hungry, and this led to him eating human flesh. After turning to cannibalism, the hunter becomes a human beast and develops an unquenchable appetite for human flesh. Since then, the transformed beast has been rumored to roam the forests of North America deep in the winter.

But a lost hunter is not all that the Wendigo is. In another version of the legend, the first Wendigo was a warrior who, in an attempt to save his tribe, made a deal with the Devil. In exchange for saving his tribe, the warrior was transformed into a cannibal. Unfortunately, his particular brand of self-sacrifice did not endear him to his people, who could not stand living in fear of being attacked by the crazed warrior. After the war, the people drove him out of the town; he was banished and forced to live as an outcast. Some legends have it that this act of betrayal drove the warrior even crazier and caused him to go on a rampage, constantly hunting for flesh to devour.

Also, it is believed that a Wendigo is created anytime a human being succumbs to their cannibalistic tendencies to survive. Hence, a transition to a Wendigo usually followed an act of cannibalism. Such transition is sometimes very rapid, while in some people, the transition is gradual, covert, and can be disguised for a while. This irreversible transition is perceived by the Algonquians to happen quite a number of times as there was a lot of hunting activity that kept people out, especially during the cold weather. Old Indians and settlers often found themselves stranded out in the cold and sometimes ate human flesh to keep themselves alive.

In the version of the legend that identifies the Wendigo as a spirit and not a creature, it is said to be a spirit that possesses human beings who are extremely greedy and display extreme gluttony and hunger. In modern literature, it is believed that this last version is mainly moral rhetoric aimed at discouraging gluttony in human beings and fostering a sense of discipline in children and adults alike.

Where Does the Wendigo Call Home?

The Wendigo, that chilling embodiment of hunger and despair, is said to inhabit the most remote and desolate corners of North America. Its alleged territory stretches across the northern regions of the United States and into the vast wilderness of Canada. The folklore emanates from the Plains and Great Lakes Natives and some First Nations. It was based in the East Coast forests of Canada, the Great Plains of the United States, and the Great Lakes region of the United States and Canada. The people of these regions are ethnologically identified as speakers of Algonquian family languages.

The creature and, indeed, the spirit of the Wendigo dwells prominently among the Algonquian-speaking tribes in Native America. Algonquian languages are a subfamily of the indigenous languages of the Americas. Speakers of the language stretch all the way from the east coast of North America to the Rocky Mountains in the northernmost part of Western Canada to New Mexico in the Southwestern United States of America.

Clearly, the legend of the Wendigo has its deepest roots in the northern regions of America, where it seems that humanity is often put to the test during harsh and extreme winters. The legend seems to have found roots among the tribes in these areas, including the Ojibwa, Cree, Innu, Salteaux, and Naskapi peoples, partly because the legend seems to be the only explanation that they have for the rise in human cannibalism during a difficult period in their history and partly because the legend offers an emotional connection to their land and the dangers present therein.

Among these tribes, the legend served as a cautionary tale, a reminder of the dire consequences of succumbing to the dark urges of hunger and desperation. The remote and untouched wilderness of Canada provided the perfect backdrop for this legend to flourish. Its dense, snow-laden forests and frozen rivers became the eerie stage upon which the stories of the Wendigo played out. Tales of encounters with this malevolent spirit were passed down from generation to generation, becoming an integral part of the oral traditions of indigenous cultures in the region.

However, as we have already established, the Wendigo's influence was not limited to Canada alone. Its chilling presence extended into some regions of the

United States, where the forests of Massachusetts, Illinois, and Delaware held their own dark secrets. Here, the legend of the Wendigo blended with other indigenous beliefs and found its place in the folklore of Native American tribes like the Ojibwa, Menominee, and the Cree.

Etymologically Speaking: What is the Wendigo?

To truly understand the essence of the Wendigo, one must explore its origins not only in the realms of folklore and legend but also through the lens of etymology. The very name "Wendigo" carries within it a wealth of cultural and linguistic significance, offering insights into the creature's nature and what it represents to the people of North America.

The term, despite its many variations, already carries some connotations as to the fearsome and cannibalistic nature of the Wendigo. The term Wendigo seems to be an anglicized version of the *Ojibwe* word "wiindigoo". In other Native American languages, such as Cree, the word is one variation or the other.

Some etymological evidence suggests that the translation of the word from Ojibwe or Cree means "fool." Some etymologists have argued that this might be some error of some copyist and that the true translation is indeed "ghoul". Yet some scholars maintain that the word is indeed the same one used to refer to fools and drunks and describe persons considered "head-heavy", and no translation error has occurred. Their justification is hinged on the fact that the monster is associated with serious mental impairment, and so the original meaning of the term is "fool".

The new sense of the word, as we have come to understand it today, would only come later with the extreme food shortages that drove people to act like cannibals. These food shortages lasted for over one hundred and fifty years, and over that period, a much-needed semantic evolution followed. You should note, however, that some researchers are still reluctant to accept the meaning of the word to be "fool" or "ghoul". To this group, the word has a more semantic affinity to "owl". The belief is that the shift was from "owl" to "cannibal" and that the characteristic of the owl as a spiritually significant predator bird makes this translation probable.

It is worthy of mention that the term "wendigo" is so deeply entrenched in the North American psyche that beyond the folk stories and popular culture commercialization of the term, the term has also been used to mark the North American landscape. In Ontario alone, there are over thirty places with the word "Wendigo" or "Windigo" in their name. From Wendigo Lake, Wendigo Point, Wendigo Beach, to Wendigo River, it seems the people of Canada cannot get enough of the Wendigo.

Not the Wendigo?

In the complex tapestry of mythological beings that populate the world's folklore, it is not uncommon for creatures to share certain traits or characteristics, leading to confusion and misidentification. The Wendigo, with its chilling reputation, is no exception. Like many mythological creatures, the Wendigo bears some resemblance to other mythical beings. Conflating the Wendigo with many of these other creatures is quite easy.

Hence, to conclude this chapter, I shall make a humble attempt to paint a clear picture of all that is not the Wendigo. This, I believe, will help you draw a more accurate mental picture in the coming chapter, where I start to tell you all that we know about the Wendigo.

Wechuge

The Wechuge is a cannibalistic monster in the legends of the Athabaskan Beaver Indians, also native to North America. Unlike the Wendigo, which one becomes by becoming too greedy or hungry, a person transforms into a Wechuge by being too powerful. But like the Wendigo, it also hunts people to eat by luring them away from other human beings and taking advantage of their desires and weaknesses. The Wechuge is described as being very cunny and intelligent, and powerful. A person could also become a Wechuge by breaking a taboo. But this is not peculiar to the Wechuge alone. A person can become a Wendigo by breaking cultural taboos and rendering themselves spiritually weak. Acts like attempting to communicate with spirits or attempting divination without being spiritually equipped to do so can make a person susceptible. A person may also be targeted for a Wendigo attack after wronging someone who can effectively wield the spirit, like a shaman.

The taboos that could make a person transform into a Wechuge is a long, inexhaustive list that makes most people vulnerable. For example, it is said that doing things like eating meat with flying eggs with it, taking a picture with a flash, or listening to music made with a stretched hide (e.g., guitar music) all constitute taboos that would trigger a transformation. Physically, the Wechuge is made of ice, unlike the Wendigo, and it can be killed by being thrown into a fire to melt overnight.

The key to avoiding the Wechuge phenomenon seems to be avoiding the space around a powerful person so as to avoid violating their personal taboos, which are connected to their power. In Beaver folklore, an old person is generally considered to carry more power than a younger person. An example would be the story of an old man who did not like his pictures to be taken with a flash. When a white woman attempted to take his picture, he covered himself up with a blanket and retreated to the back of his tent. If the man's picture had been taken regardless, he would have transformed into a man-eating beast unable to control his own desires or judgment.

A person who has begun the transformation into a Wechuge can be cured halfway through the transition. The curing process is done by enticing the power of the "giant-man-eating-animal-spirit" to leave his body and return to its place within the medicine bundle. If a Wechuge is not cured, it will begin to eat his own lips, and this will turn to ice within him. The final stage of the transformation will be the Wechuge eating human flesh.

The only way to get rid of a transformed Wechuge is by its own death. When the Wechuge dies, it ceases to exist naturally. The only other way, as mentioned earlier, is for it to be burned in a campfire. In Athabaskan folklore, the Wechuge phenomenon is associated with the presence of strangers in the community who are not familiar with the taboos of a person's medicine bundle and power. Generally, there are fewer reports of a complete Wechuge transformation. In fact, the scholar credited for most of the research on the Wechuge phenomenon, Professor Robin Ridington, reports only one full Wechuge transformation. This has been linked to the fact that Beaver Indians generally did not mix too much with strangers and outsiders, which could have triggered a transformation.

Kwakiutl Man Eater

The Kwakiutl Man Eater is another legendary man-eating giant spirit that bears some resemblance to the Wendigo. The Kwakiutl Man Eater represents the basest desires of man, which he learned to reject through socialization. The ugliness of the creature is representative of social deviation.

Like the Wendigo, the Man Eater is related to overwhelming hunger, which must be tamed for social good. The most significant difference between the myth of the Wendigo and the Man Eater is the initiation process, which signals an acceptance of the personality of the cannibal monster, during which the individual is firstborn of the cannibal monster and then tamed so that the monster's power is integrated in the personality. An initiate possessed by the Man Eater becomes a cannibal dancer. The dance is used to symbolize a transition from the spirit world of uncontrolled hunger to the human world of control. The ritual is used to establish the fact that no matter how overpowering the feeling of hunger is, morality will always prevail.

Oni

In Japanese folklore, a creature that acts typically like our Wendigo has been the subject of many works of literature and art. The Oni is a type of demon that, like the Wendigo, dwells deep in the mountains and forests. The Oni are characterized by superhuman strength and an evil nature that manifests in their insatiable desire for human flesh. However, physically, the Oni bears no close resemblance to the Wendigo, with its hulking figure serving as a sharp contrast to the Wendigo's gaunt figure. The Oni have horns growing out of their heads, massive teeth, and a third eye in the centre of the forehead. The Oni, like the Wendigo, can sprout yellow skin but unlike the Wendigo, it can also appear in many other colours, such as blue, black, green, and red.

Alongside its evil nature, the Oni is associated with controlling forces like thunder and lightning. Oni can change their shape and form to mirror the weaknesses of the victim and lure them to their destruction.

Chapter 2

UNVEILING THE WENDIGO

"The Wendigo was gaunt to the point of emaciation; its desiccated   skin pulled tightly over its bones. With its bones pushing out against its skin, its complexion the ash-gray of death, and its eyes pushed back deep into their sockets; the Wendigo looked like a gaunt skeleton recently disinterred from the grave. What lips it had were tattered and bloody ... Unclean and suffering from suppuration of the flesh, the Wendigo gave off a strange and eerie odor of decay and decomposition, of death and corruption."

- Basil H. Johnston (The Manitous)

We have already established in the previous chapter that any information you are getting about the Wendigo largely depends on who you are asking. So, you might come across some contrasting features and characteristics of the Wendigo in this chapter. However, I think I must establish first that one non-negotiable physical feature of the Wendigo is its ugliness. Unlike the Japanese Oni, which oscillates between extreme ugliness and alluring beauty, the Wendigo is ugliness personified.

Some legends describe the Wendigo as an emaciated, skeletal figure covered with ashen flesh. The creature is deemed to be gaunt to the point where an image of bones jutting out of flesh is a common depiction of the legend. On the other hand, some legends describe the creature as a giant creature or beast of up to fifteen feet. In Ojibwe, Eastern Cree, Westmain Swampy Cree, Naskapi, and Innu lore, the Wendigo is a giant many times larger than human beings. In this description of the Wendigo, it grew bigger and larger the more flesh it consumed. Hence, every time the Wendigo ate a person, it would grow to the size of the person so it could never be full and would always be on the hunt for the next person to eat.

The Wendigo's eyes also have varying descriptions. In some accounts, which tally with the earlier description of the creature as gaunt and emaciated, the eyes of the creature are sunken deep into its socket, rolling uncontrollably as they follow its victim. In other accounts, the eyes of the creature are vibrant and glowing as it reflects the fear of its victims. The fearsome look of the creature is complemented with sharp yellowed fangs and claws, which it uses to hunt. In an uncanny similarity to the Wechuge, the Wendigo also doesn't have full lips either because it has chewed them in or completely eaten them.

The Wendigo is reported to have a heightened sense of smell, sight, and hearing characterized by pointed ears. The Wendigo may also sprout horns or antlers like a deer. As a reflection of its diet, the approach of the Wendigo is often detected through an overpowering smell of rotting flesh, which alerts humans of its presence in an area.

Whether gaunt and skeletal or hulky and built like a beast, the Wendigo, in all accounts, is reported to have superior strength and speed that allows it to stalk its victims and catch up with them if they try to escape. The speed of the creature is not altered by deep snow or ice. It is unclear whether this is a result of adaptation to its natural habitat or physical advantage bestowed by the shape of its feet. Typically, the Wendigo is found in colder areas among the woodlands and lakes of Canada and the northern parts of the United States.

Since the Wendigo is a human transformed into a beast, it may retain some of its human characteristics, such as the ability to recognize people or speak. In some legends, the Wendigo converses with its victims, telling them frightening stories to threaten or taunt them before attacking.

In some other versions of the legend of the Wendigo, the creature has the ability to use tools, survive partial dismemberment, and eat parts of itself without dying. This version is reported by Lottie Chicogquaw Marsden, an ethnographer of the Chippewas of Rama First Nation. In this particularly chilling account of the creature, the Wendigo can wield and use a knife. The account reads thus:

> "One time long ago, a big Windigo stole an Indian boy, but the boy was too thin, so the Windigo didn't eat him up right away, but he traveled with the Indian boy, waiting for him till he'd get fat. The Windigo had a knife, and he'd cut the boy on the hand to see if he was fat enough to eat, but the boy didn't get fat. They travelled too much. One day, they came to an Indian village, and the Windigo sent the boy to the Indian village to get some things for him to eat. He just gave the boy so much time to go there and back. The boy told the Indians that the Windigo was near them and showed them his hand where the Windigo cut him to see if he

was fat enough to eat. They heard the Windigo calling the boy. He said to the boy, "Hurry up. Don't tell lies to those Indians." All of these Indians went to where the Windigo was and cut off his legs. They went back again to see if he was dead. He wasn't dead. He was eating the juice (marrow) from the inside of the bones of his legs that were cut off. The Indians asked the Windigo if there was any fat on them. He said, "You bet there is; I have eaten lots of Indians, no wonder they are fat." The Indians then killed him and cut him to pieces. This was the end of this Giant Windigo."

Legends hold that the only person who can destroy a Wendigo or at least control its powers is a shaman wielding silver, steel, iron bullet, or a dagger but historical accounts show otherwise. The wendigo has been overcome by ordinary men of extraordinary courage. It is also sometimes believed that Shamans can transform a person into a Wendigo by placing them under a curse. Some other legends, such as the one quoted above, claim that the Wendigo can be overcome by cutting it up into little pieces, while some others claim that the heart of the creature specifically must be cut out and melted or burned in a fire before the Wendigo can be truly destroyed.

In cultures where the Wendigo is identified as a spirit rather than as a physical creature, the features of the Wendigo differ. For example, in Cree mythology, it is believed that the Wendigo is an evil spirit that can possess a human being by biting such a person or by coming to them in their dreams. The person who has been possessed then begins to act violently, attacking people and eating human flesh. A person who is gluttonous or greedy is believed to be susceptible to being possessed by the spirit.

I Am Hungry, The Wendigo is Near!

The prominent belief among the cultures where the Wendigo phenomenon is alive and thriving is that a person once possessed by the Wendigo spirit would transform into a monster that eats people. This transformation is often marked by intense violent urges and a strong desire for human flesh. Hence, a person who has been possessed by the spirit of the Wendigo can often tell what is happening to them. Oftentimes, this awareness was a source of frustration that fuelled further predisposition to violent outbursts and fear. Such was the case of a woman named Marie Boucon from a

Cree community. Not only did people in her community believe her possessed by the malevolent spirit and plot to kill her, but she herself lived in fear of what she might do to others because of her "transformation".

Word of the plan to have Marie Boucon murdered reached the police, who took her away to safety to live in a mission house. During the winter of 1990, Marie, surrounded by the Sisters in the mission house, seemed to have become calm and outgrown her fear of causing harm to others until the day she realized her protection amulet was gone. Even though Marie had been involved in the mission's activities and faithfully consuming gallons of holy water, she could not help but fear that she would succumb to her cannibalistic desires once the amulet that the Cree people believed stopped such transformation was gone.

But long before Marie Boucon, the Wendigo has lent itself to some interesting symbolism within North American sociology and politics. The association of the creature or spirit, as the case may be, with extreme hunger and starvation was exploited by the Canadian government in putting the Native Americans and their lands under its control. Hence, there was a period in history marked by widespread Wendigo hysteria, with many Algonquian peoples believing themselves to be transforming into the Wendigo. By the nineteenth and twentieth centuries, there was a wave of state-sanctioned murders of people believed to be undergoing a process of transformation. What this illustrates is the great significance that hunger and, by extension, a scarcity of resources played in the legend of the Wendigo. Aside from hunger being a symptom of the phenomenon, it also appears to be the cause.

Hunger is a central theme in the Wendigo legend. Those who are prone to gluttonous behavior are deemed by the indigenous communities as predisposed to going Wendigo. Those who cannot control their greed live in the constant threat of an ill-fated transformation into a wendigo. However, one must note that although hunger is a central theme in the legend, it is not necessarily an essential element. Meaning that a person could have plenty of food and resources and still go wendigo. This category of persons would experience symptoms such as an aversion to normal food and would generally be unable to recognize food as edible. Instead, they experience an intense craving for human flesh.

Dreams and Possession

"He says his heart is freezing. He is always saying that he is going to be a cannibal.... He wants them to kill him all the time before he gets worse.... He seemed to be getting worse all the time. He does not look like a human being. He seems to be terribly swollen in the body and face. I do not know how this will end. The sight of him is enough to frighten any person. ... The sound of him was terrible. He was calling like a wild bull".”

- **Francis Work Beaton (1897)**

In indigenous traditions, dreams are such a powerful cultural and spiritual tool that people rely on in making judgment calls and making decisions. Among many Algonquian tribes, the prevailing belief is that dreams are indications of what would happen in the real world, and sometimes, they place bigger premiums on these dreams as dreams are believed to be spiritual revelations. Dreams are believed to make people more powerful by giving them a glimpse into what is to come. Hence, people who dream often or can interpret dreams often have a respectable disposition within their communities. Generally, dreams do not imply impending doom, although, in the context of our discussion, dreams foreshadow an undesirable transformation.

Aside from uncontrollable hunger, another telltale sign that a person is doomed to become a wendigo is that they have dreams that indicate that they are under a spiritual attack. Many people who have turned Wendigos often report vivid and powerful dreams of transformation right before they undergo such transformation. According to traditional beliefs, if a person dreams of becoming a Wendigo, then there is a real danger that they would become one themselves. These dreams are typically filled with images of ice, cold, and blizzards. After a person starts to have these dreams, it is believed that their situation can still be remedied through certain rituals and traditional offerings. These rituals are believed to have the ability to stop the transformation. Unfortunately, they are not always successful, meaning that despite a person's best efforts, if he is doomed to go Wendigo, no ritual song or sacrifice can stop it.

Like in many traditional African and Asiatic traditions, the Algonquians also believe that if a person who is experiencing such dreams allows himself to consume food, usually game food offered by the Wendigo spirit in the dream, he will be possessed by the spirit. Getting tempted by food leading to something more sinister is a very common theme in folklore globally, and the tale of the Wendigo is no exception. In the case of the Wendigo, the meat it offers is usually human flesh disguised as ordinary game food. In an account reported by George Nelson of the HBC, he retells the story of a man whom the spirit of the North and Ice (signaling the spirit of the Wendigo) had come to in his dreams.

The Cree people found these spirits particularly malignant and as signaling trouble. Nelson writes: "These two they are much afraid of because they are both highly malignant spirits; there is no joking or jesting with them. Those who at any future period are to become cannibals dream of them." In the dream the Cree man has, he sees the North coming to him with a series of dishes. The first dish was a duck. He was about to eat it when a stranger sitting next to him nudged him and told him not to eat the dish. It was only then that he saw that what seemed like a duck to him was actually the arm of a child. But the spirit of the North was relentless. And so the spirit offered him meat, which also turned out to be the flesh of other Cree. Yet the spirit tried again; it offered the man hearts, which he also refused. The spirit of the North, realizing he could not succeed in turning this man in his dream, commended him, saying: "It is well done—thou hast done well." It then became obvious to the man that had he eaten what was offered to him as food, he would have become a man-eater. ''Heh! Had I unfortunately eaten of this then, had I become a cannibal in addition to all my other misfortunes.'', The grateful man quipped to Nelson.

The Wendigo spirit combines two powerful forces that would spell death for any person: hunger and cold. Hence, once a person experiences the dreams of cold and has had his hunger satiated by the flesh offered by the Wendigo spirit, the spirit then possesses them. The Wendigo spirit targets people in a state of spiritual weakness, which is usually marked by hunger and the hardship of the winter. Spiritual weakness may also be caused by a person committing a taboo or an unacceptable spiritual or cultural act or by being a victim of a targeted spiritual act.

A person possessed by the Wendigo spirit will experience a desire for human flesh. Sometimes, this does not come with the desire to kill people, just a desire for their flesh. In a possessed state, people will start to look like game animals, so they cannot necessarily tell the difference between committing murder and killing game. A possessed person will not always stay in their crazed state; they are bound to experience moments of lucidity in between, but the longer they stay possessed, the farther and in between these moments of clarity are. They also go through periods of extreme melancholy, and they withdraw from society, stop eating, and stop speaking to people, often out of fear that they will harm them.

The possessed goes through periods of extreme emotions, oscillating between manic possessed states where they become extremely violent to extremely melancholic states. At this point, the cannibalistic urges become harder to control in the possessed, and they withdraw further because they are fearful of harming their loved ones. The possessed would often exhibit super strength, making it increasingly difficult to subdue them. Legend has it that old women who go wendigo are often the most difficult to control as they are far gone in the process of possession before anyone takes notice because they are often underestimated. In one report, it was said that about fifteen men were required to take a possessed woman to be committed to an institution.

Beyond the super strength that the possessed now seems to have, there are also visible physical changes that reflect what they are undergoing. In some cases, they start to swell, growing bigger and larger in the body and the face. Before a possessed person acts on their cannibalistic urge, there is a chance that they can be cured. However, the transformation becomes irreversible once they act on their wanton desires.

Ice and Isolation - The Wendigo's Chilling Domain

"The elemental conflict of man against a hostile nature has nowhere been enacted more dramatically than in the experience of the Ojibway Indians of southwestern Ontario and northern Minnesota, where the hunter, isolated by his vast lands and frozen winters, felt himself a soul at bay, against cosmic forces personalized as cynical or terrorizing."

- **Ruth Landes (Ojibwa Religion and the Midewiwin)**

In the haunting legends of the Wendigo, there is a stark and unforgiving backdrop —the landscape of ice and isolation, which pushes all the boundaries of survival and sanity to their limits. When it comes to the Wendigo, even the elements of nature conspire to test the resilience of the human spirit. Starting from the home within which the Wendigo spirit lies — the northern forests of Canada and the frigid expanses of the northern United States set the stage for this chilling legend. Winters here are long, brutal, and unrelenting, with temperatures plummeting to bone-chilling depths.

The wilderness is vast, the snow-covered terrain seemingly endless, and the silence is deafening.

This, coupled with the way of life of the people necessitated by the extreme weather, sets the stage for a Wendigo possession. Communities in these areas often find themselves cut off from the outside world for months at a time, their only company the howling wind and the endless expanse of snow. The people often have to break into small sub-units to be able to hunt for food to eat. In such isolation, the mind can become a breeding ground for fear and paranoia, but is the wendigo just about paranoia? I think not. It is within this isolation that the Wendigo finds its fertile ground. As food becomes scarce and the cold gnaws at the bones, the line between friend and foe can blur. The very fear of starvation, combined with the relentless cold and isolation, sets the stage for a period of spiritual weakness that characterizes a wendigo episode.

Yet the ice theme in the legend goes beyond this alone. The Wendigo itself embodies the natural forces that shape its domain. Its skeletal form reflects the physical deterioration brought about by extreme cold and hunger, while its icy eyes mirror the unforgiving winter that surrounds it. It is a creature born of the very elements that define its world. Additionally, victims of the Wendigo often describe themselves as feeling like their hearts or backs were turning to ice, literally. People around them can hear their chests sounding like ice popping under pressure or the sound of ice crunching and scraping. Legend also holds that when a Wendigo has been killed or dismembered, their hearts are usually found covered in ice. Rituals such as burning the heart for the ice to melt away must be carried out to fully get rid of the spirit and ensure it does not resurrect.

Another way in which ice is relevant to the Wendigo legend is that during the period of possession, the indigenous peoples of North America believed that one way to reverse the transformation was to force the victims to drink hot tallow with the hopes that the hot fat will melt the ice forming around the victim's heart and help them lose their cannibalistic desires.

Wendigos have a strong connection to the winter, and because they are most active during this season, they are believed to have some control over blizzards and snow. It is very rare that a person will become possessed by the spirit during the summer. They have a connection to ice not just spiritually but also physically as well. Aside from the Wendigo's heart being encased in ice, its skin is always freezing cold, and its spirit sometimes dwells in ice, necessitating the warning that people should not eat ice or make snowmen out of it for fear that they may become possessed through it.

Sceptics have attributed the notion that children should not eat ice to some moral injunction to prevent children from playing in dangerous weather. George Nelson, an employee of the Hudson Bay Company, which was a strong European force in North America in the seventeenth century through to the mid-twentieth century, in reference to the way the natives perceived the Wendigo said: "They fancy that the blood which circulates thro' the heart first forms into water, then coagulates or congeals into solid and imperforable or impenetrable ice."

Water and ice are the Wendigo's natural habitat, and it is where it shows the most strength and agility. A person caught by a wendigo in icy conditions cannot outrun the creature, which can simply glide through the ice. In fact, it is said that the Wendigo can breathe underwater and live in ice and at the bottom of icy cold lakes.

Shape-Shifting Giant Monster and Cries of Death

> "Its breathing is like the whistle of a train, audible for miles, and its shouting weakens the limbs of the Indian it pursues."
>
> - **Diamond Jennes (1886-1969)**

As we have established earlier in this book, the Wendigo is sometimes regarded as a giant who keeps growing to the size of his victims. But this narrative, anthropological evidence would suggest, is one that only takes root in the distant past, set majorly in the memories of the indigenous tribes as the wendigo withdrew from their lives. In fact, there is a widespread belief that the last of its kind was run over by a train sometime in the nineteen sixties. However, just because these giant monsters are presumed to be long gone from these parts of the world does not preclude the possibility that they might exist someplace else, living out a different kind of history.

Yet the narrative of them as giants is highly probable. The activities and escapades of the Wendigo are inconsistent with that of a regular-sized human being or that of a gaunt, skeletal figure. For example, in a reported tale, a hungry Wendigo attempts to use its power to stop a moving train and eat its passengers. Although the Wendigo is run over by the train, it is likely that the creature who attempted such a feat is one who relied on its appearance to have some paralyzing effect on the crew.

But how do we reconcile these two consistent yet contradictory accounts of the bodily structure of the Wendigo? To this writer's mind, the earlier explanation offered as the Wendigo undergoing different stages in its life cycle still lends itself useful here. A Wendigo spirit might start out as the gaunt, fiendish creature that many have described and only grow to a giant size with each victim it consumes. Also, the Wendigo is believed to have shape-shifting abilities, so it is possible that the creature transforms itself from a giant beast to a gaunt, skeletal figure and vice versa.

The stories indicate that the Wendigo can control its size, often swelling up to when it was on a rampage and shrinking down in calmer times. It is also believed that they have the ability to transform into owls such that a sighting of an owl among the tribes might be taken to mean that the appearance of a wendigo was afoot. Another animal believed to be subject to the mystical control of the Wendigo is the sharp-spined porcupine.

Porcupine

The conditions within which the Wendigo lives are also one that is hard to reconcile with a human-sized creature. The weather conditions are extremely harsh, and the Wendigo is perpetually on the hunt. It is not far-fetched that it would transform into a beast that signals doom. The etymological connection of the Wendigo to owls renders it to the narrative that, like the owl, the creature foreshadows some kind of bad omen, such as the fact that someone would die. The proto-Algonquian word for wendigo, wi-nteko-wa, means owl among the Meskwaki, Miami-Illinois, and Cheyenne tribes. But the connection does not end there. The anthropologist,

Robert A. Brightman, is of the opinion that the piercing gaze of the owl is just like the cold-blooded stare of the Wendigo that many Algonquian natives have reported. What is unclear from this narrative, however, is whether the reference to the evil was the attack of the Wendigo itself or a death that was connected to something else outside the Wendigo.

Another factor that makes the Wendigo such a fearsome creature is its cry. Aside from its pervasive stench, this is one of the first telltale signs that a Wendigo was coming. Many of those who have witnessed a wendigo rampage at some point describe it as a terrible cry, a high-pitched wail very much like a loud whistle. In some narratives more in tune with the description of the Wendigo as a giant, the sound is a bellowing sound that moves the ground beneath the Wendigo and all that surrounds it. So shocking is the cry of the Wendigo that all those who hear it go into temporary shock, become unconscious, or are unable to move or do anything meaningful or requiring thought for minutes.

Moss Traps and What Not

You might be wondering what Moss, nature's velvet, which covers the earth with its miniature emerald forests, appearing even in the remotest parts of the world where life is bleakest, has to do with our monster friend, the Wendigo. Well, moss and lichens, more often than not, feature prominently in the Wendigo lore. Before delving into the physical significance of the plant to the legend, it is worthy to note that the moss is sometimes used as a symbol to represent the "spreading pestilence that clings to things and parasitically feeds off whatever it comes in contact with. Its parasitic nature is analogous to the wendigo spirit by the way it possesses and clings to victims, devouring their minds and slowly encasing their hearts in ice".

Beyond this, natives believe that the Wendigo has the power to control moss, causing it to grow in its wildest forms in order to use it as a snare to capture its victims. Also, when human flesh is unavailable, it is believed that the Wendigo relies on moss for sustenance until its next victim comes along. Hence, it grows as much moss as it can, eating some and leaving some to use as a trap for the next human being that wanders to its abode. This earned the Wendigo the sobriquet "moss eater". If a person is suspected of going wendigo, the people would often check their teeth for remnants of moss to see if they have taken to the diet of the Wendigo spirit as well.

A move away from the spiritual and symbolic would lead us to a more science-based relationship between the moss and the Wendigo. In their book, Wendigo Lore: Monsters, Myth, and Madness, Chad Lewis and Kevin Lee Nelson offer a nutritional connection to the plant. According to the authors, there is a species of the lichen plant called the "smooth rock tripe" which the indigenous tribes refer to as the "windigo wakon" (wendigo cabbage). They describe the plant as very bitter and as a last resort starvation food that has to be soaked and boiled over and over again to be edible. If not prepared properly, the wendigo cabbage can cause extreme bowel issues, nausea, and allergy symptoms. The writers then propose the hypothesis that it is possible that some of the cases of wendigo sickness reports of "swelling up" and loss of appetite for normal food could have been a reaction to eating unprepared moss and lichens and that allergic reactions to toxins contained within rock tripe may lead to a state of delirium, causing victims (and witnesses) to believe someone was going wendigo. But the authors also caution that we must "view this information within a broader cultural context". There might be more to the wendigo cabbage than this caution suggests.

Kettles and Families: Wendigo Narratives and Themes

Across the diverse indigenous tribes in North America, the narratives surrounding the Wendigo are as varied and complex as the cultures themselves. Within these intricate stories, we find threads that speak to the essence of human existence, touching upon themes such as sexuality, family, women's roles, and the everyday objects that fill their lives. The legend of the Wendigo often weaves multifaceted tales, where the creature represents not just hunger and despair but also the imminent fear of losing one's sanity in the unforgiving wilderness.

The family bond is central to many Wendigo narratives, serving as a powerful backdrop against which the struggle for survival and the battle against inner demons are played out. The subject of family plays out in many different ways across different narratives. The legend often explores the dynamics of family bonds and the lengths to which individuals will go to protect their loved ones from the Wendigo's curse. These stories emphasize the importance of community and the sacrificial nature of familial love.

In some narratives, family serves as a force of resistance against the evil creature. In some others, family structure is the target of the spirit. In these tales, Wendigo represents a threat to marriage and other forms of familial relations, fertility, and gender roles. For example, when a wife deserts her husband, the Wendigo is used as a weapon to destroy such an erring bride; a powerful shaman father uses the Wendigo to punish his daughter who has eloped with a man; and there is the brother-in-law who uses his sister-in-law as bait to lure out the Wendigo.

Water spirits, too, make their appearances. In these narratives, the Wendigo takes on the character of a water spirit and lures his victims into the river to meet their doom. This particular narrative is evidence of the constant evolution of the legend of the Wendigo. The reduction of the "giant" to a water spirit is a reflection of societal evolution. Over time, indigenous peoples became more connected and intertwined with Europeans and their religion. As they became more exposed to European culture, tales of a giant that ate people began to fade from the mainstream but not totally from the psyche of those who have experienced the Wendigo phenomenon for centuries. Hence, the evolution of the Wendigo to a spirit that dwelled underwater. With Christianity and "civilization", the indigenous peoples did not stop believing in the wendigo; they merely changed its character to suit their new belief system.

In some Wendigo narratives, the creature served as a symbol of sexual taboos. The Wendigo's insatiable hunger is often equated with a lustful desire that defies social norms. These stories caution against the consequences of unchecked passions and the importance of respecting cultural boundaries. Also, sexual violence played out in these narratives, such as when a captured Wendigo is forced to eat the phallus of its dead victims by their spouses.

The role of women in indigenous tribes is often intertwined with the symbolism of cooking and food production. While both genders participate in food production, the role of preparing the food mostly falls on women. In some narratives, kitchen utensils that women use are regarded as symbols of destruction for the Wendigo. For example, it is strongly believed that a kettle, a pestle, or a sewing bag can destroy a wendigo completely.

Madness is also a recurring theme in Wendigo narratives, reflecting the profound psychological impact of isolation and the harsh wilderness. The fear of madness, both as a result of encountering the Wendigo and as a consequence of the creature's curse, serves as a potent reminder of the fragile boundaries of the human mind. Also, most people lived in constant fear of what the creature could do to their minds, and this fear in itself sometimes caused them to act irrationally.

The Wendigo, in all its terror, multiple identities, and complexities, serves as a canvas upon which these communities paint stories that explore the complexities of human existence, the role of women in society, the fragility of sanity in isolation, and the enduring strength of familial and communal bonds. These tales are not merely cautionary; they are a reflection of the resilience and cultural heritage of indigenous peoples. In the next chapter, we will explore many of these tales and some documented stories of the Wendigo.

Chapter 3

WHEN "THEY" MET THE WENDIGO

The only way supernatural creatures become a subject of human investigation, and attention is through calculated appearances that they make to people. Sometimes, people have claimed to have figured out ways to lure mythical creatures out of hiding. While this might be probable, it is more likely that these mythical creatures choose the people whom they want to behold their presence. If it were the case that people could simply lure out mythical creatures if and when they wanted, then the world would long have descended into chaos. With the number of legendary creatures that exist, it would only be a matter of time before the world went crazy under their collective influence.

Hence, when someone claims to have been favoured by a legend with their appearance, their claims are scrutinized and treated with a healthy dose of initial scepticism before the respect and awe that comes with confirming some elements of their stories (there is no way to verify an encounter with a supernatural creature completely).

When legends come to life before people's eyes, curious individuals like you and I owe it as a duty to posterity to breathe life into those stories by telling and retelling them as much as the boundaries of plausibility will allow. We also owe a duty to find ways to protect the originality of these tales and not water them down with our own interpretations and assumptions. In this chapter, I shall attempt a fulfillment of this duty by telling you some of the recorded stories of the Wendigo.

The Jesuit Encounters

Paul Le Jeune, a Jesuit missionary, writes of an early encounter with the Wendigo. Le Jeune, who had begun his life as a Calvinist and protestant, had become a catholic priest and was sent on an evangelization mission. On his mission to New France, he observed a woman experience the Wendigo and was shaken by the encounter.

In his writings, Le Jeune describes a woman who, one night in 1636, in an area known today as Quebec, had entered a shaking tent that was built to communicate with the spirits. The tent shook so violently that Le Jeune was scared that she had caused the devil to come. The report states that when the "devil" came, it came to warn the locals against the local Algonquins and

Montagnais from settling with the French. The Spirit, or was it the devil, warned that it had eaten some Attikamegouekhi, a group of native tribes and that he would eat more of them if he were not called elsewhere. If he couldn't, he would send an Atchen (Wendigo) in his place who would eat them and the French as well.

The encounter appeared to Le Jeune as a ploy to keep the missionaries from settling among the natives as they were preparing to do. The prior strategy of the missionaries and the French in converting and colonizing the natives was proving ineffective as they soon realized how much they needed them to survive within these territories. The initial imperialist arrogance of the Europeans was lost in the reality that they could not survive or make any meaningful strides in these communities without showing some respect for their way of life.

The missionaries relied on the natives for basic things such as food and shelter and could not take a high-handed approach as they had been doing in other communities. Soon, the cultural life of the natives, which, unfortunately for the missionaries, included the Wendigo, became a part of their mission as well. Hence, it became inevitable that the Jesuit missionaries would have more experiences of the Wendigo. In Trois-Rivières, Quebec, there was a terrible famine during the winter of 1634 - 1635. During that period, Father Jeune met with a man who claimed that his brother was refusing to eat and was going mad. His wife and sister-in-law, fearing that the brother might turn on them, were planning to get rid of him. The man who has become of the church was in a moral dilemma as to whether killing his brother would amount to a great sin. Father Jeune instructed the man to hide all weapons, such as spears and axes, within the house, which his brother could use to harm any member of the family.

This episode shows that indeed, the Jesuit missionaries were connected to the legend, and they documented their interactions with the natives, which involved the Wendigo, creating the first set of evidence as to the beliefs of the Algonquian people. But what is also worthy of note is the fact that the missionaries did not take any proactive steps toward getting rid of the creature. They remained as impassive spectators in such deeply emotional and cultural affairs of the Natives

Another documented interaction of the Jesuits with the creature occurred in 1661 when the Jesuits were planning a major meeting with the people of Northern Quebec. They had chosen the Lake St. John (Lac St. Jean), a major rendezvous spot for the Algonquian-speaking tribes. The Jesuits, in preparation for the meeting, sent emissaries to the location to gather all the people for the meeting. Unfortunately, they were all killed

The Jesuit fathers Gabriel Druilletes and Claude Dablon arrived at Lac St. Jean (now in Quebec) in mid-June 1661 to the information that their intermediaries had met their deaths in a rather strange manner. "Those poor men ….. were seized by a species of disease, which affects their imaginations and causes them a more than canine hunger. This makes them so ravenous for human flesh that they pounce upon women, children, and even upon men, being unable to appease or glut their appetite — ever seeking fresh prey, and the more greedily they eat. This ailment attacked our deputies, and, as death is the sole remedy among those simple people for checking such acts of murder, they were slain in order to stay the course of their madness".

The Jesuits, doubtful of the news they had received and dismissing it as some of the ways of the "savages" they were interacting with, decided to proceed with their journey. But they too would have unusual experiences within their travelling party that would cause the belief that the "epidemic" that killed the emissaries had followed them too.

French Officials and Hudson Bay Company Officials

HUDSON'S BAY

INCORPORATED 2 MAY 1670

It was not just the missionaries who were in Quebec who had reports of the Wendigo; other officials working for the French Government in the area also interacted with the creature indirectly. A French surveyor named Joseph Laurent Normandin reported an instance where a female wendigo was murdered in 1732. According to Joseph, the wendigo was killed near an area called Chicoutimi, Quebec. The locals still revered the spot and continued referencing it in discussions about the creature.

The Hudson Bay Company was a fur trading company with powerful influence among the natives from the eighteenth century into the mid-twentieth century. The company remained a powerful force largely because fur trading was a major economic activity that sustained many indigenous peoples.

Records from this company showed some strong Wendigo activity during this era. In a similar trend, officials from the North West Company, another fur-trading company with a great deal of influence, also point towards several Wendigo encounters. Some of the encounters recorded by the charter companies are particularly gruesome, while some are so lacking in details that we would be disregarding them altogether.

One often reproduced encounter is one that happened in 1823 on what I assume would have been a very spooky Valentine's Day Eve. George Nelson, an HBC employee from Lac La Ronge, Saskatchewan, a place with its own share of scary monsters and flying saucers, kept records of Wendigo encounters during his time at the HBC.

At three on the evening of February 13, 1741, two Cree women had a very strange encounter with Wendigo. The women were both suffering from starvation and had come down the river at Fort Churchill, Manitoba. The daughter, speaking to the HBC employees in the area, told them that she had a family of her own before. Her family, that is, her husband and three children, had run out of food, and in response, her husband, who was a goose hunter for HBC, killed and ate the youngest child and, days later, moved on to another son. In fear that the man would eat them all, the woman took her eight-year-old daughter and tried to leave with her mother. Unfortunately, the man caught up with them and throttled the girl while she was in her mother's arms. The woman who told the story evidently was able to escape, but none of her children did. She and her mother eventually overcame the husband-turned-beast and axed him to death.

While it is easy to disregard this story as the story of a starved man who turned to cannibalism to survive, further investigation into the period and context within which this story happened will reveal that it might have been a little more than that. According to the HBC factor, Richard Norton, the man who turned on his family, could have easily hunted animals with the tools and vigour he had about him. At the time of the carnage, "[W]hat is very surprising at ye time of this Disaster there was Plenty of Deer (caribou) about them & he had ammunition & might have killed Venison which his family Strongly desired him to do, but he gave no manner of Care to their Solicitations, but his mind seemed to be fixed upon what is above related ..."

However, one might want to take Norton's observations lightly. After all, he was a man sheltered from the realities of the natives who lived around him. Yet regardless of what Norton or any other person's opinion might suggest, the natives to which this happened seemed to think it was a lot more than hunger that forced this man to turn on his children as meals.

In another case reported in 1774 at "Severn House (now Fort Severn, the northernmost community in Ontario), an indigenous employee of the HBC had threatened to stab his wife to death and kill many other locals. The locals reported him to the HBC, enjoining the officials to kill the man. The company and its enlightened officials would rather not make such a decision, so they had him confined in chains. However, in these times, the fear of a wendigo or a perceived wendigo often defied all diplomatic solutions. So, the locals took matters into their own hands and killed the man themselves. It is worth noting that the HBC employees did not try to stop the men, and this goes to show that beneath the detached air of superiority and civilization that the Euro-Canadians and their English superiors displayed, deep within them, they recognized the fear of the natives. Also, the attitude of the employees of the company varied depending on their rank and level of education. It was not uncommon to see an uneducated employee of the company sharing the "superstitions" of the native Indians.

This type of situation continued to play out at different HBC posts. Another recorded tale shows a similar event at York Factory, which was a key HBC post in an area that is now part of Manitoba. In April 1978, the natives brought what looked like a man afflicted by some disease of the mind to the trading post. In those times, HBC ports often served some social function beyond their economic relevance. These ports often served as a place where locals could go for food and medical treatment. This made economic sense because anything that significantly affected the locals was bound to affect their trade in some ways.

The man who had attempted to kill some people before being brought to the fort soon escaped, causing a great dilemma. News that the man had escaped was bound to cause great distress among the people because, as the HBC factor in the post put it, "even the idea of having a madman on the Coast — will alarm the natives for many miles — and the very name of one being within several days journey from their hunting ground will occasion that quarter to be deserted for some years — and my fear is that our goose hunt will suffer in consequence of this man's escape...". While it appears that the factor's major concern was their "goose hunt", it must be noted that the significance of the man's escape was not lost on him either. He sent out hunting parties to look for the man. When word of the man's escape got to the Crees, they threatened to kill him on sight. There is no record to show that the man was ever found after his escape, but locals believed he must have met his death somehow.

In the Winter of 1900, HBC traders at Rupert House had a rather scary experience with the Wendigo phenomenon. In a journal of the house found years later, it was recorded that on February 12, 1900, eight Cree men who all looked very skinny had come to buy provisions. On Friday, 16, 1900, three local Cree men arrived just before dinner. The arrival of these men turned what would otherwise have been a beautiful, uneventful day into a day marked with dread. The story goes:

"Frank, Blue Boy & William arrived before dinner. Richard hung himself on (Wednesday) the Man went mad on Monday. (Simon) and William were the only two men in the tent they had a dreadful story to tell, he seemed to get a supernatural power, he wanted to kill and eat the children, they had to rush out of the tent and make a fire in the woods, it was so cold and stormy they nearly perished with the cold, William threw him a (line) with that he finished himself, his miserable wife wanted the men to finish him with an axe, my only regret is that it was Richard in place of his wife, who is a bad woman …"

Even though from many of the accounts recorded, it would seem like the HBC officials and traders did not quite understand the fear that the natives had of people they considered merely "mentally ill", they were not immune from the effects that the fear of the creature could have on their trading activities. Take, for example, in 1845, at Oxford House, Manitoba, a local spiritual leader claiming that his spiritual friends had sent him a message about some dangerous person traveling through the country and killing all Indians he could find caused ripples of fear to run through the locals. The housemaster, George Gladman, recognizing the gravity of the situation, said, "I am doubtful whether I shall by any means be able to allay or dispel this absurd panic; if not, they will do no more in fur hunting for the remainder of this Season; which is much to be regretted as I expected 200 Mbr, (Made beaver) from the exerting of such good hunters as they are, during the next month." By the end of that week, many locals had come to the port seeking safety.

In the interest of their business, Gladman had to take proactive measures. Partly to reassure the natives that all was well and under control and get them back to work and perhaps partly because he needed to reassure himself that their fears were baseless. He sent out strong warrior men to look for the beast, and eventually, they brought back news that there was no trace of a beast in the wilderness, and the spiritual leader lost his credibility among the natives.

The belief that the natives were blinded by their superstitions was one that really took root among the officials, and they acted in a way that signalled that they did share the cultural beliefs that made the Natives squirm in fear. This sometimes translated to "reckless" behavior, such as taking in people feared to be Wendigos or in the process of transformation into Wendigos. For example, in 1838, an HBC employee, Richard Grant, took in a woman who was brought to him by her Cree brother-in-law. The woman was reported to be deranged and believed in her mind that she would be going wendigo and turning into a man-eater.

In another situation in 1888 at another HBC post, the Eastmain post. The post was not of particular economic significance to the company, but it served as an important source of food for trapped ships. The point was mainly used to keep cattle and was exposed to the "bleak northwest winds off the sea". The post, therefore, was quite the trouble for HBC. A Cree man, in particular, had a chequered history with the post. Apparently, the man was part of a family that had attacked one of HBC's posts at Hannah Bay, Ontario.

The man, Peetawabano, had, at a moment of extreme starvation, done an act that he at the time probably considered self-sacrificing but which truly amounted to the undoing of his family.

That winter, the family suffered such extreme starvation and hunger that he drained his own blood into a cup for his family members to drink for sustenance. The only member of the family who did not participate in this "blood feast" was the daughter-in-law. One of Peetawabano's sons, who drank the blood then descended into unimaginable realms of violence and madness that drove him to kill Peetawabano himself and set off a chain of mindless killings in the family. In the end, Peetawabano and his wife, four brothers, their wives, and grandchildren were dead. The daughter-in-law, who refused to drink the blood, somehow escaped with her own child and, by February 1888, showed up at the Eastmain post.

When the woman arrived with her tales of cannibalism, it was hard to believe. Fortunately for her, but not quite so for the other members of her family, Peetawabano's youngest son, a sixteen-year-old teenager with eyes wizened by human flesh and violence, appeared at the post in March 1888. The teenager refused to eat regular food and, after being questioned by officials at the post, admitted that he ate human flesh and had killed some of his family members in the immediate past.

The arrival of the young man at the post understandably caused some excitement among the locals, and Corston, the HBC boss at the post, was forced to make a decision. It did not seem like Corston would have done anything of the sort of exposing the young man to the authorities for a trial or anything at all were it not for the fact that the man's presence was interfering with life at the post. But again, it was clear that Corston considered all of this superstitious and thus proceeded to take the young man into his home against the will of the locals in Eastmain. Again, Corston's main concern was economic. Hence, the fur that the family had gathered was his focus.

George Nelson Accounts

While George Nelson is an HBC official who worked in North America during the height of the Wendigo phenomenon among the native tribes, it might serve more historical significance to tell his stories separate from the others. The singular reason for this is that Nelson's records reflect a willingness and curiosity to understand the beliefs of the Natives among whom he operated and lived, and thus, his encounters are presented with a perspective lacking the condescension in which the other officials recorded their encounters with the Wendigo.

George Nelson was an HBC employee in Lac La Ronge, Saskatchewan, around 1823. George Nelson, displaying an attempt to understand what was going on around him, writes: "They have such a dread and horror of this that it is constantly on their minds." George recounts the sort of wishful envy with which the Natives regard him as a white person who lives as he pleases without the wendigo caring much for him or bothering him. The natives considered themselves being continually troubled by the Wendigo even though they do all that they can to drive him away from them.

One significant way in which Nelson's accounts differ is that he is of the opinion that the natives are in "general kind and extremely indulgent to those thus infected: they seem to consider it as an infliction and are desirous of doing all they can to assist." Other accounts from HBC officials leave the impression that the natives were quick to castigate those who were turning Wendigo and quickly tried to put them to death. According to Nelson, families of those who were afflicted by the Wendigo spirit of madness tried to treat them, and sometimes they succeeded.

Nelson recounts tales of instances where a person has been completely cured of the spirit and returned to normal life. One of the stories that Nelson tells is of a father who started to transform into a Wendigo around 1812 or 1813 and was cured of the spirit. The father would stare intensely at his daughter, gushing about his love for her. He would say: "My daughter! I am fond of thee! I love thee extremely." The woman would reply: "I know thou dost". And then her father would go: "Yes! I love thee—I think I could eat a piece of thee; I love thee so much."

The daughter whose mother was dead was with her husband, who stood by her during these moments. Usually, after dark, her father would undress and, making strange noises, would walk out of their tent and lay upon a heap of wood curled up like a dog. Each time they (his daughter and her husband) tried to bring him back into the tent, he would refuse. He did this for a month, refusing to eat anything except raw meat. Eventually, the man would make a turnaround, and he "became, as usual, composed and good-natured."

In another instant, a young girl who had just gotten married got seized by the Wendigo spirit. The girl became so violent that the men stopped leaving the tent in order to protect other women and children from her wrath. Fortunately, the young bride makes a recovery as they cropped her hair short. The girl, upon recovery, says she has no recollection of all that they said she had done. In her words: "I do not recollect any single one circumstance of all that it told me — I thought I was always on the tops of the Trees."

NaPaNin

When four men armed with an axe gather around a single man who is without a weapon, and yet he gives them a tough time, it is kind of obvious that such a man does not act on his strength alone. Sometime in January 1896, a 35-year-old man named Napanin set out from Wabasca to visit his father in Trout Lake. The man who is known by members of his tribe to be a responsible man who provided well for his family and was in fairly good shape before setting out on the journey suddenly develops a strange behavior. The man was traveling with his wife and children, and the trip went well up to the second day when the wife reported that the man was acting strangely, saying that some animals were trying to attack him.

No one in the travel party could determine what was after Napanin or cause him to act so scared. His wife became worried about his behaviour and then pushed him to travel ahead of the rest of the family. It is speculated that she was fearful for her life and her children's lives. The woman also seemed to be under the hope that the man would get help from the rest of his tribe when he arrived at Trout Lake ahead of them. Unfortunately, this was not the case as Napanin progressively worsened, and his body started swelling. In addition to this, Napanin continued to display more fits of madness that were terrifying for all who witnessed it.

In moments of lucidity, Napanin would beg his family members to kill him if he became dangerous. Napanin's death came when one day, his wife went out with children, and four men who were called in to secure Napanin with ropes became threatened by his attempts to wriggle free. They struck Napanin to death with an axe and then burned his body to get rid of the wendigo completely. Napanin's death was reported in the May 8, 1896 edition of the Glenboro Gazette.

Marie Counterville

Watching a family member or loved one fall sick and deteriorate is a painful feeling no human being ever wants to go through. It is an even more painful experience where what has gripped your loved one is a sickness of the spirit that makes you an attractive meal to them. And then there is the possibility that as they continue to succumb to whatever it is that is eating up their body or soul, the responsibility of finally pulling the plug on them would fall on you.

We, as students of history, can only imagine the levels of trauma and pain that Marie Counterville's family went through in that ill-fated summer of 1887. But their trauma, it seems, might not match Marie's as she watched all her seven children and husband die one after the other. Although Marie remarried, she never did get over the consistent blows that fate delivered to her. Marie moved away to the Slave Lake area, but that did not mean she could escape the cruel hands that were already dealt her. Marie and her family were a part of a larger encampment of natives who were living near the confluence of the Lesser Slave River and Lesser Slave Lake just outside of Alberta. For weeks, Marie was under the stronghold of the Wendigo spirit that drove her to and from the brink of madness and cannibalism. The natives watch as Marie descends into a terrible state. It seemed like her weak emotional and spiritual state had made her susceptible to the evil spirit of the Wendigo. Marie stopped eating and was in an extremely subdued state for a long while. However, the changes that Marie was undergoing were not limited to her mind alone. Her body began to swell as further evidence of the Wendigo spirit in her life. As Marie continued to suffer spiritual and physical pains, her worried husband, Michael, expressed to her his fear that she was becoming a cannibal, to which Marie, who was not oblivious to what she was going through, said: "It is to be that I aim to eat you. I like you all, but I am bound to eat you---kill me, for I intend to eat you."

Marie's obvious affection for her husband could not stop her from wanting to kill him and eat him. In the same vein, Michael's affection for Marie stopped him from killing her, despite the fact that she was an obvious threat to his life. If this wasn't some book about a monster, this would have made for an epic love story to retell. To protect Marie and obviously himself and his son, Michael hid all the weapons in the house. Whenever the household was asleep, Marie would look around for the weapons so she could "make a meal" for herself. Eventually, they had to have Marie bound, and despite the fact that they tried everything to cure her, Marie continued to go through this gruesome transformation.

Marie continued to lash out violently at those around her, and eventually, Michael would have to do what he feared the most — killing his own wife. For a while, Michael and his son prayed, hoping to avoid having to let Marie go. When it became clear that if

Marie was not killed, she would transform fully into the cannibalistic beast, Michael summoned some courage, grabbed two axes, and smashed her head and breasts in. The spirit that had taken hold of Marie took a while to let go, and her body was reportedly moving for over an hour before she died.

Unfortunately, Michael and his son had committed murder in the eyes of the law, and their altruistic intentions were no excuse before the law, so they were sentenced to years of hard labour in prison.

Moostoos

The wave of wendigo cases and their murders inevitably brought with them a wave of court cases where the men who took matters into their hands were tried. Like the men who got rid of Marie Counterville, the men who would eventually put the Moostoos affair to rest would also have to face a court of law for their actions. The murder of Moostoos was so brutal that their trial made it to newspapers across the world. But before we get ahead of ourselves, the question we should be answering is: How did they get to court in the first place?

Thirty-two band members were camped together at Smoky River near Lesser Slave Lake in Northern Alberta. Despite the obvious hardships and deprivations of the winter, the band members still lived together peacefully and were bound together by a spirit of brotherhood that was rare during times of extreme hunger and brutal cold. Regardless, the band stayed together, and all seemed to be well until Moostoos, the star of our story, started to complain to his people that "he was afraid an evil spirit was getting the better of him and that he would turn Wehtiko". The man, perhaps at the time already overcome by desires of cannibalism, warned his band members to get rid of him should he ever go wrong (try to kill someone to eat). Moostoos was particularly scared of harming his own children and tried as much as possible to fight the changes that were happening in his mind and body. But soon enough, it wasn't just Moostoos who was plagued by something — a strange sickness started to plague the rest of the tribe.

Moostoos and some others were taken to the chief medicine man of the tribe. A man called Entominahoo who tried to cure Moostoos of whatever had possessed him. Yet as the days rolled by, Moostoos took on a more frightening appearance, and he started to say things like: "I look on these children as young moose and long to eat them." With Moostoos looking more dangerous than ever and uttering statements such as this, the tribe knew it was only a matter of time before Moostoos turned on them. In an attempt to bring Moostoos back to reason, they constructed a special medicine lodge where they enlisted all their spiritual skills and power to help Moostoos. From sundown to almost midnight, the rituals carried on, with Moostoos lying quietly on the floor.

Suddenly, Moostoos yelled into the night: "This night you will all die," thrashing about like a man possessed by a force greater than him. Eventually, Moostoos got up and yelled at all present, "I will kill you all; I will not leave one alive." This was the moment that the people of the tribe realized just how far gone Moostoos was.

No one of those who were present could boldly say that he did not fear for his life as Moostoos started running around the room, trying to tear at people like some wild animal. Eventually, a woman in the crowd identified as Eliza struck Moostoos with her medicine bag while a man named Chuckachunk smashed his head with an axe she handed him. Another member of the tribe, Napaysoosis, also stepped in and drove a knife into Moostoos body and stuck the axe in his chest. Another man named Payoo also struck Moostoos in the chest with an axe. For one man, this was all too many blows.

Throughout the night, members of the band watched Moostoos bloodied body, half-expecting him to spring back to life so they could kill him again. The party, still unconvincing of Moostoos destruction, drove a stake through the axe hole in his chest and poured a boiling liquid into the open wound. This act reflects the belief of the natives that a wendigo's heart was made of ice. This overly gruesome act appeared to be an attempt to thaw the "icy heart of the Wendigo". Again, as day broke, they tied up the body in chains and attached them to two pickets in the ground, rendering his dead body immobile. But they did not stop there; Napaysoosis chopped off Moostoos head before they left the body tied to a chain in a picket in the ground.

With the way and manner in which they got rid of Moostoos, it appears like it was not just Moostoos who had some coldness in his heart. At trial, only Napaysoosis was sentenced to prison, and since the murder of Moostoos was widely considered to be an act of self-defense, he was sentenced to just two months imprisonment with hard labour.

Eating Creek Road Monster

In 1992, a newspaper editor named Joe McWilliams wrote about the Wendigo. In coming up with his report, Joe spoke with some residents of Eating Creek Road who had heard stories of the giant man-eating monster in the area. The article reports a local legend about a giant man-eating Wendigo who lived among them. The area of the report was an encampment along Eating Creek, where a small trickle of water joins Mitsue Creek and then goes on to the Lesser Slave River. The people in the area lived in constant fear of what the beast would do to them. The beast was always on the hunt and looking for the next person to devour. Soon enough, its presence in the creek became common knowledge, causing many Natives to avoid the place and warn others against trading or moving around the area. Unfortunately, beyond Joe's report, there are no further details about the monster's activities in this area. The only thing we can be sure of in this story is that the name of the road is a reference to the residents' belief in some monster activity in the area at a particular period.

The Swift Runner

The Swift Runner

If you believe in destiny, it would not be such a wild claim to say that the Swift Runner's destiny was to bring one of the biggest terrors of the Native peoples to the limelight. Before the Swift Runner, the Wendigo phenomenon was not something a lot of people outside the tribes had heard about. But when a respectable member of the community makes a three-sixty turn and murders his whole family, the world is bound to pay attention.

Swift Runner (Kakisikutchin) ((Kaki-si-ku-chin) was an educated Cree Indian who traded with the Hudson Bay Company in the Athabasca region of Alberta, Canada. He was also a guide to the North West Mounted Police and was considered very intelligent, although he had what was generally considered an unusual fondness for whiskey. At the time of the incident, it was estimated that Swift Runner was just about forty years old, was married, and had six children. Like many other natives, during the winter of 1878, Swift Runner was travelling with his family looking for food. He was on the trip with his mother, brother, wife, and their six children. The hunt for food was going on well initially, and Swift Runner was able to get enough game to feed his family. Unfortunately for Swift Runner and his family, the brutal cold of the winter pressed on, and there were fewer animals to hunt. Before long, their reserves dried up, and the family had to keep moving to find food to eat.

But that could not possibly be the end of Swift Runner and his family, could it? Well, it was sort of the end for his family members because their reserves drying up set off a chain of events that would lead to their deaths. However, for Swift Runner, the end was a little further down the road and a lot more dramatic than death from starvation would have been. By Spring of the following year, Swift Runner would go into a mission house in St. Albert, telling an incredulous tale about how his entire family had died of starvation and only he braved the cruel winter. Despite the fact that Swift Runner was well-known by the authorities and the locals in the area, not many people believed this tale of his. It was not easy to accept that a man whose entire family died starving looked as well as Swift Runner did, and their incredulity at his tale might also have something to do with the fact that Swift Runner could have tried to approach the HBC for food since his camp was just about 25 miles from them. Either way, the police got involved, and the man was asked to account for the rest of his family.

Begrudgingly, Swift Runner led the police back to his camp so they could check out their remains and confirm his story. On the trip back to the camp, it became obvious at some point that Swift Runner was merely going around in circles with the policemen and the rest of the search party. Eventually, it was Swift Runner's love of Whiskey that would be his undoing. The police gave him 'muss-kee-wah-bwee' (alcohol to which a large quantity of plug tobacco was added) and that did the trick on him. Before long, Swift Runner was telling on himself and showing the police what was left of his family — their bones scattered all over the winter quarters.

It was definitely not just the bones that gave him away now; it was also the fact that the bones were broken into smaller pieces and the marrow completely sucked out, kitchen utensils in the camp held remnants of human flesh, and all these seemed normal to Swift Runner as he walked around casually picking up skulls and giving the rest of the party a tour of his quarters. According to newspaper accounts of the incident, Swift Runner nonchalantly introduced his family members to the party by identifying their bones. The police gathered up the bones as evidence and buried what they couldn't carry before leaving the area.

The reports differ on some of the details of how Swift Runner admitted to the murder of his family members. In some accounts, Swift Runner simply told the rest of the party and the police what happened without much prodding. In another widely repeated account, Swift Runner made his confession to a French Catholic Missionary in St. Albert, Father Hippolyte Leduc, who ministered to him in his last days. According to Father Leduc, Swift Runner claimed that he was camped in the woods with his family when he fell sick, and those around him could not find anything of note for them to eat. Soon, they had to kill their hunting dogs and survive on their flesh till they ran out. When he recovered from his illness, Swift Runner said he went to an HBC post and got some provisions, but it didn't take so long for that to run out as well. He said his brother and mother set out first to look for some meat, and he stayed back with his family even though they had nothing to eat. Then Swift Runner asked his wife and children to follow his brother's tracks in search of some food. He hoped that even though he was still weak from his illness, he could support himself alone. With all his family members gone except one of his boys, who was about ten years old at the time, Swift Runner tried hunting for food. Unfortunately, nothing came out of any of his hunting trips, and they both suffered extreme hunger. And then one morning, Swift Runner looked upon his son lying down, weak from hunger, and he saw in his son the solution to his immediate hunger.

Swift Runner shot and killed the boy and then cut him up and survived on his flesh and marrow for days. Some days after, with renewed strength, the Swift Runner was wandering about in the woods when he came upon his wife and other children and told them that the boy who remained with him had died of starvation. His family told him they had not seen his mother and brother, and it seemed like they had died of starvation because, by then, months had passed. Note that many accounts implicate the Swift Runner in the deaths of his brother and mother, with some accounts even going as far as reporting that the Swift Runner complained that his mother's flesh was tough. After reuniting with his family, the Swift Runner's oldest boy dies, and they bury him (the police found his grave and evidence of starvation in his emaciated bones during the investigations). To stay alive, they had to boil some pieces of their leather tent, their shoes, and robes.

The Swift Runner claimed to have uncovered some plot by his family to leave him in the woods, and he woke up one morning extremely mad, and it seemed that all the devils had entered his heart. Supposedly pushed by the devils now in his heart, he shot his wife and hacked his three daughters to death. He was left with one little boy who was the last surviving member of the family. He sent the boy to make water from snow as he made meat from the rest of the family, extracting their marrow and brains. All this flesh, however only took them about seven to eight days, and then he left his last surviving son.

Eventually, the dreary winter was over, and spring came. The Swift Runner, afraid of coming in contact with people and having them figure out that he had killed the rest of his family, stayed away from people. He started to hunt for game again, and they kept living in isolation until the devils took over his mind again and told him to kill his only surviving son and ate him like the others. While we can attempt to explain the Swift Runner's initial actions in the context of extreme hunger and famine, his act of killing his last son, even when there was game available for hunting and he had, in fact, hunted some, is baffling. Could it be that truly the devil (Wendigo) lived in the Swift Runner, as he claimed? Or could it be that the Swift Runner was suffering from mental illness, or could it be both? That is, a mental illness caused by the Wendigo?

Regardless of why Swift Runner did what he did, he had to face the consequences of his actions, and when brought to trial, the jury was swift in running him to the gallows. There are many questions as to what happened to his body after he was killed. Some accounts claim that he was immediately buried in the snow nearby, some accounts claim that his body was just dumped, and some are of the opinion that the natives had taken control of the Swift Runner's body and burned it to melt his icy heart. Whichever it is, the man was gone, as was all his family members.

Chapter 4

AM I CRAZY?

While researching this book, one recurring thought to me was about just how much of the wendigo stories could be about a mental illness and not some spirit or monster that dwells in the woods in the winter. Admittedly, when it comes to folklores and legends, the lines between reality and imagination often blurs and because most of these narratives we have happened centuries ago, there is the very real possibility that a lot of things have been lost in history, translation, and time. Yet, we would be hypocrites not to even consider the very real possibility that the subject of this book exists only in the collective imagination of a group of people who have had to brave extremely cold winters without any of the tools of modern technology that we have today all the while experiencing extreme hunger and deprivation.

This type of thing is what psychologists would call a culture-bound syndrome. According to the American Psychological Association, a culture-bound syndrome (or culture-specific syndrome) is a pattern of mental illness and abnormal behaviour that is unique to a specific ethnic or cultural population and does not conform to standard classifications of psychiatric disorders. Culture-bound syndromes include, among others, amok, amurakh, bangungut, hsieh-ping, imu, jumping Frenchmen of Maine syndrome, koro, latah, mal de pelea, myriachit, piblokto, susto, voodoo death, and windigo psychosis.

However, we must be careful in this theorizing not to present an assumption that the Wendigo phenomenon fits conveniently into one cut of the earth and is restricted to the people in that area. The Wendigo phenomenon is alive and present beyond areas we would consider part of Native America. The term Windigo psychosis was coined by Dr. John Cooper, an anthropologist at Catholic University who theorized about a condition in which the "victims imagine themselves actually to be the dreaded 'Witiko,' which has a heart of ice and lives on human flesh." Examined within the context of psychology, the Wendigo psychosis represents a manifestation of how people's environment can influence their mental ills.

Some of the symptoms of the disorder are hallucinations, convulsions, melancholia, insensibility to pain, catalepsy, and, of course, an intense desire to consume human flesh. Further research into the illness introduced different new perspectives, such as the fact that there might be a nutritional angle to the ailment. The people of the First Nations regularly went through periods of extreme hunger and starvation. This lack of nutrition, Vivian Rohrl suggests, might be responsible for symptoms such as nervousness, fatigability, changes in disposition, vague digestive disturbances, and anorexia. And that using tallow as a remedy only proved effective because tallow was rich in fat and vitamins that might eliminate the symptoms.

Yet, the Wendigo psychosis is not the only explanation that has been offered to dismiss the Wendigo phenomenon. There is the theory that what has been recorded in history as the Wendigo phenomenon is just an extreme case of Seasonal Affective Disorder (SAD). The idea that the whole legend is a ruse for powerful tribe members to get rid of those who are weak among them or to get rid of perceived enemies has also been proposed. So has the notion that the phenomenon might be an extreme manifestation of a physiological disorder. Infections such as measles, smallpox, influenza, and other infectious diseases were very common at the height of the wendigo phenomenon, and they ravaged the indigenous peoples. These diseases have all been linked to severe delirium, and when you consider the fact that healthcare and vaccination were not available, it might be easy to understand why infections might take such a toll on a person before anything is done about it.

As logical as all these conclusions sound, we cannot present them as the answers to all the questions that this book has raised. In fact, each of these explanations presents further questions of their own. A lot remains unexplained.

Chapter 5

The END OF THE BOOK ABOUT AN UNENDING LEGEND

How to Kill a Wendigo & The Wendigo Today

As my ink dries up and the pages of this book thin out, I feel I must end this journey on a certain note. I tried to give you answers to questions that you might have as factually as possible, but even I realize that for the curious mind, the end of this book offers them new challenges and new barriers to overcome. The world, or at the very least parts of it, will always be shrouded in a chilling mystery. Defeating a Wendigo is not an easy task. In fact, it is a task that no one in the modern day should take on. Thankfully, it seems like the Wendigo no longer bothers itself with us humans. I might think that climate change might have a little something to do with that. I mean, Mother Nature has been showing how dynamic she can be lately, and we as humans are not really helping douse the tension between us and her.

Wendigos, when found in the past, were killed by axe and then burned so their icy hearts may melt. And because it is believed that the Wendigo can grow back, its head used to be severed from the rest of its body to prevent it from coming back to life. It was also destroyed using silver or steel objects. All of these seem like solutions that can only remain present in our works of history and fiction — not to be attempted.

In contemporary culture, the Wendigo continues to hold a prominent place in horror literature, film, and other forms of media. This is not so surprising. The wendigo phenomenon offers the imagination no boundaries to tap into the themes of isolation, mental illness, cannibalism, and the lives of the people who lived long before us.

The Wendigo frequently appears as a terrifying antagonist in horror novels, short stories, and graphic novels. Authors such as Algernon Blackwood, Stephen King, and Graham Masterton have all featured the Wendigo in their works. The Wendigo has also been depicted on screen and in video games both as a traditional supernatural creature and as a metaphorical representation of psychological torment. Some contemporary artists even use the Wendigo as a symbol to explore themes of cultural identity, colonialism, and the preservation of indigenous traditions.

In conclusion, the Wendigo remains an enduring phenomenon in the realm of horror and folklore. While it has evolved and adapted to fit modern narratives and sensibilities, its roots in indigenous culture and the primal fear it represents continue to captivate audiences and storytellers alike. With the Wendigo, it would seem the possibilities of danger and art are limitless.

Other Titles By G.D. Pickering

Mysterious Creatures: American Cryptids

Mysterious Creatures: British Cryptids

Mysterious Creatures: European Cryptids

Mysterious Creatures: The Michigan Dogman

Mysterious Creatures: The Mothman of Point Pleasant

Mysterious Creatures: Terror in The Swamp (Boggy Creek Monster)

Mysterious Creatures: The Legend of The Loch Ness Monster

Mysterious Creatures: Cryptid Encounters

Mysterious Creatures: Cryptid Encounters Volume 2

Mysterious Creatures: Cryptid Encounters Volume 3

Mysterious Creatures: Cryptid Encounters Volume 4

Mysterious Creatures: Cryptid Encounters Volume 5

Mysterious Creatures: Cryptid Encounters Bigfoot Special

Mysterious Creatures: Cryptid Encounters Dogman Special

Mysterious Creatures: Paranormal Encounters

Available ONLY on Amazon.

Social Media

Email your encounters to

Mysteriouscreatures2022@gmail.com

Follow us on YouTube here

https://www.youtube.com/@mysteriouscreatures2022

Follow our Facebook Page here

https://www.facebook.com/Mysterious-Creatures-117257113515156

Join our Facebook Group here

https://www.facebook.com/groups/970443407051105

Printed in Great Britain
by Amazon

49087317R00056